GET YOURSELF OUT OF DEBT NOW!
(Here's How)

JAMIE VERMEEREN
Certified Financial Planner
Financial Management Advisor

Order this book online at www.trafford.com/08-1327
or email orders@trafford.com

Most Trafford titles are also available at major online book retailers.

Note for Librarians: A cataloguing record for this book is available from Library and Archives Canada at www.collectionscanada.ca/amicus/index-e.html

Printed in Victoria, BC, Canada.

ISBN: 978-1-4251-8622-7

We at Trafford believe that it is the responsibility of us all, as both individuals and corporations, to make choices that are environmentally and socially sound. You, in turn, are supporting this responsible conduct each time you purchase a Trafford book, or make use of our publishing services. To find out how you are helping, please visit www.trafford.com/responsiblepublishing.html

Our mission is to efficiently provide the world's finest, most comprehensive book publishing service, enabling every author to experience success. To find out how to publish your book, your way, and have it available worldwide, visit us online at www.trafford.com/10510

www.trafford.com

North America & International
toll-free: 1 888 232 4444 (USA & Canada)
phone: 250 383 6864 ♦ fax: 250 383 6804
email: info@trafford.com

The United Kingdom & Europe
phone: +44 (0)1865 487 395 ♦ local rate: 0845 230 9601
facsimile: +44 (0)1865 481 507 ♦ email: info.uk@trafford.com

10 9 8 7 6 5 4 3 2

I dedicate this book to my dear wife Stacy
And my fantastic children
Kaili, Jana, Braeden,
Seth, and Sarah

ACKNOWLEDGEMENTS

To Janice McCaffery and Brian Mennis who encouraged me to reach higher and be a finisher.

To my mom and dad who always lead with love.

To my brothers Doug, Randy and Jeff who lead by example

And to my assistant Janet Harder whose enthusiasm and energy are contagious.

TABLE OF CONTENTS

PREFACE

WHY I DECIDED TO WRITE THIS BOOK

AMERICA IS MORE THAN TWELVE TRILLION DOLLARS in debt at federal, state, corporate and personal levels. Twelve trillion dollars! According to an article in USA Today, «A financial storm warning is in effect for consumers across the nation ... consumer debt is at record levels, and more people are increasingly falling behind on credit card payments. More households are seeking bankruptcy protection from their creditors...

The «alarm bells are ringing,» says Ruth Susswein, Executive Director of Bankholders of America. «Credit card debt continues to rise at a dramatic rate and incomes are not keeping pace.» (Christine Dugas, «Many Families are Living on the Edge,» USA Today, October 31, 1995).

How has this happened? Getting credit has become so easy that most people have let credit card debt exceed personal savings, putting hundreds of thousands of families on the brink of bankruptcy. Consider the following statistics. In the 1930s, at the height of the Depression, there were 70,000 personal bankruptcies in the US. Fifty years later, in 1980, the number had exploded to 315,000. Ten years later, in 1990, even that high number had more than doubled to 720,000. Two years after that, it had reached a million — and in 2002, 1,577,651 people filed for bankruptcy.

Currently in the United States over 795 million credit cards circulate: 400 million retail cards, 245 million bank cards, 120 million gas cards, and 30 million travel and entertainment cards. On these cards, American consumers charge more than $220 billion per year. The average consumer maintains a balance of $1,400 on credit card debt alone, with an average interest rate of 17%.

It should be obvious that most consumers will never get out of debt. But I did, and YOU CAN. Here is my story, and why I decided to write this book.

In September 1997, I found myself in a very uncomfortable situation. I was 24 years old, married for about a year and a half, and had a three month old daughter. I had a year left to go before I would finish my business degree, but I found myself completely out of cash. All financial reserves were drained and I was supposed to come up with tuition in a week.

As a Canadian attending a US university, I was in a tough predicament. The Canadian government was unwilling to give me a student loan because I was studying abroad. The US government would not give me a student loan because I wasn't a citizen or resident of their country. Continuing my education through the use of student loans was out of the question until I could establish permanent residency, which takes a good two years. I also couldn't get a personal loan as I had no income and no credit. I resolved that no matter what, I would finish my education.

I was lucky enough to receive a temporary working visa until my application for permanent residency was finished. With no income and no cash for tuition, my wife and I made a tough decision. We decided that she should stay home with our daughter and I would find a way to complete school and work. I was a young father with a new baby. I'd promised to do my best for my family, and frankly I was scared to death that I wouldn't be able to fulfill that promise.

I remember waking up in the middle of the night wondering how I was to put food on the table. For the first time in my life, I was entirely responsible for myself, my wife and our daughter. I didn't have money for rent, and because I young and living in the US instead of my homeland of Canada, I didn't have bad credit — I had no credit. As much as I hated it, I had to take a semester off to try to provide for the family and earn enough funds to pay tuition for the winter semester. I had four months to earn cash and plenty of it, or I knew I could never return to school and finish my degree.

I walked around campus checking out job boards. Pretty much every type of job I could find paid minimum wage at best. My wife had a couple of cousins, also attending the university, who worked for minimum wage on the custodial night shift. It was an honest living; however, I strongly believed that I had more to bring to the table than scrubbing toilets at two in the morning. Besides, there was no way I could earn the income I needed making so little. There were simply not enough hours in the day to earn what I needed making only minimum wage.

As I walked away from the job board in frustration, I bumped into one of my close friends and shared my situation with him. He told me of a debt management company, new in town, that specialized in helping families get out of debt faster. At the time I had no debt and no real assets, and as a business major with a focus on finance I was skeptical. As far as I knew, there was no way to get out of debt faster; you simply had to pay the piper, carry out your term, deal with the interest rate and do the best you can.

While having a very late night worry session, I couldn't get the debt management company out of my mind. I kept wondering how this could be possible; how could someone make a profit from paying off someone else's debt? Was there a margin? Could it be a scam? How were they making money? And more importantly, what strategies were they using that I wasn't learning in school? Could I be missing out? I've always believed that you can't win at any game until you first learn the rules. If there were rules out there, I wanted to know what they were. I had to see what they were doing.

The following morning I looked up the telephone number of the debt management firm and called them. I told them I was a university student in the business management department and I was doing a paper on a few local businesses. I asked to interview one of the managers as soon as possible, as I was under the gun for time. Maxine, the receptionist, booked me an appointment with Phil Ostler for the following day.

Phil's understanding was that I was a student coming in to write a report on their company. Frankly, I was a skeptical kid who intended to prove, at least to myself, that this man was a scam artist and this company was a fraud.

I arrived for the meeting, fifteen minutes late, in jeans and a t-shirt with a backpack on my back — looking like the student I claimed to be. Phil was kind enough to go ahead with the meeting anyway. I complimented him on his beautiful

GET YOURSELF OUT OF DEBT NOW!

office, and he asked if we could get right into the interview as he had allocated thirty minutes for me and fifteen were already gone. He also let me know we had to make it quick, as his next appointment was with a serious investor. I pulled out my notepad and began to ask questions: How is it possible to make a business helping others manage debt, and what do you do to help them? Over the next hour and a half I threw questions at him like a javelin. We talked about consolidations, debt stacking, negotiating with creditors, pulse paying, etc. I was fascinated. We went back and forth on questions and I challenged his responses. I was stunned to find out what was available and how to take advantage of different opportunities I didn't know existed. I then asked him what someone working for him would get paid. He told me that for those working in the debt management department, specifically those working directly with clients, earn $1300 per case, or about $300-$500 per hour.

Almost without thinking, I shot out my hand. "Sounds good, I'll see you for training on Monday." He was floored. In confusion he extended his hand in return and I gave it a good firm shake before walking out of his office and into the hallway. What just happened here? Phil never offered me a job; I never asked for a job. I had no intention of asking for a job. I was so embarrassed at my audacity that I stood in the hallway wondering if I should go back and apologize. But what would I say? After hesitating in the hallway for about thirty seconds, I decided perhaps I should just leave.

As I walked through the reception area on the way out, I spotted a visibly irate man — the investor Phil had mentioned as being his next appointment. He was furious that Phil had kept him waiting for over an hour. I felt I should apologize for taking so much of Phil's time, but I didn't. I walked right past him and left the building.

When I got home and told my wife what I'd done, she looked at me like I was crazy. Then we both laughed and I asked, "What should I do?" Should I show up on Monday? And if I did, what if Phil laughed me out of the building and sent me home? He certainly had every right to do that. But on the other hand, what if I could earn $300-$500 per hour and not have to do the midnight shift scrubbing toilets. This would help me provide for my family and allow me to finish school. After all, what could I really lose? I decided I had to take the chance.

Monday morning I arrived at 9 am with my best suit on, not sure what to expect. The woman at the reception desk asked me to wait, as Phil was busy. I nervously flipped through magazines in reception for about forty minutes before Phil came down with a couple of other professional looking people. I could hardly believe it when he introduced me as their newest debt management consultant!

I shook their hands and spent the day going through PowerPoint presentations on the ins and outs of the debt management program. Needless to say I fell in love with the job. I loved the idea of families arriving absolutely stressed out, many in tears, and within a couple of hours I could give them practical ways to get out of debt. No more bill collectors calling, no more feelings of hopelessness. In almost 90% of the cases, we could help them avoid bankruptcy through a proper plan, and this company administered the debt program for them. In the worst of scenarios, even if bankruptcy was the final result, we could face it head on and get them on their way with a renewed hope in a better future.

What I loved about it was the creativity. There was never one way to look at a problem. What if we consolidated? Oh, credit is not good, perhaps we can pulse pay. What if we restructured this or that? How do we avoid or minimize penalties or refinance costs? Ah, they've missed a couple of payments; this could give us more negotiating power with the credit card company. No two situations were the same. Each situation brought new solutions.

A couple of weeks later, I was at a family dinner with my wife's cousins (the toilet cleaners) and they asked what I was doing for work. When I told them I was a bankruptcy and debt management consultant they thought I was joking. They reminded me that I didn't yet have my degree; who would hire me for this type of position without a degree? After all, they got better grades than I did and they were scrubbing toilets.

For the next couple of months I worked for the debt management company part-time in the evenings while I finished my degree.

After I graduated, the company asked me if I wanted to do some contract work brokering loans for the US Military Veterans Affairs. I thought the job would look good on my resume, and Phil generously agreed to fly my now-pregnant wife and daughter along with me so we could be together.

I was also excited about the idea of traveling and working in different cities. The idea seemed more of an adventure than a job and I jumped on board. The idea was first discussed on Friday afternoon and Sunday night I was in a hotel room in Denver trying to figure out what a VA loan was. I had that night to familiarize myself with the software and terminology as appointments were lined up the following morning.

I took a shuttle to Arvada, CO where I met Rex Vaugh. He

gave me an overview of the software and handed me a completed file. "This is what they are supposed to look like," he said. The key was to get the Veteran Affairs Certificate — 20 signatures, 17 initials — print out a good faith estimate of the costs, and include a copy if their land title, survey, etc., etc., ad infinitum. If I missed any of the required signatures or paperwork the loan would be kicked back and rejected. Because we were traveling to different cities every three weeks, the chance of an incomplete file being fixed would be slim to none. Did I understand? Of course not — not entirely — but the next morning I was doing the "fake it, 'til you make it" routine in front of the client.

For VA loans there was one way, no creativity. Families would come in. I would ask them the same question every time. Do you want to lower your monthly payment or decrease the time left to payout the loan? Inevitably families wanted to lower their monthly payment. After that I would run the same ratios, process the costs to complete the loan, and I could tell them within thirty seconds if it would work or not. After that we collected and processed the same paperwork again and again. Over time the passion was gone. I went from being very creative to mechanical.

Once I figured out what I was doing, my brain went on autopilot and I could do this in my sleep. We would joke that the paperwork we were completing didn't matter to the processors or government, only that it weighed a certain amount. If the paperwork weighed 3 lbs they let it go through — if it only weighed 2½ lbs they kicked it back. The job was much different than before. No creativity. There were no unique ways of looking at a problem. There was one way, and it wasn't much fun.

With interest rates on the rise loans were getting harder to close, and with our second baby on the way, living three weeks a month out of a suitcase was not the life Stacy and I saw for ourselves. We decided we wanted to find a place to settle down. Stacy really wanted to move back to Canada to raise our children around family, so we made the change.

When we moved back to Canada I wanted to find a career where I could get out of the mechanical mode and into something that could be creative and fun again. I felt I needed a career where I could make a meaningful difference in the lives of others. I found that Canada's debt management programs weren't the same as the ones in the US. There were some who claimed to do debt management, but they seemed far more like bankruptcy agencies and credit counselors to me. Many of their consultants didn't have the instincts or knowledge to really help. There was one not-for-profit credit counseling service that focused more on budgeting, but I could find no other company that dealt strategically with prevention and remediation.

What I really wanted was a job where I could feel I was creatively helping people. A family friend, John Swenson, the Vice President of National Banks, was kind enough to make calls to banks on my behalf and help me set up interviews. I met with four of the six major banks in Canada and wasn't satisfied. In each case, I felt I would be pigeonholed into one area of banking only to have to fight to get into another area where I would be equally pigeonholed. The personal touch seemed to be gone. The idea of churning people through a process like cattle wasn't something that made me passionate about my job. I interviewed with a couple of venture capital firms, who looked at my age and pretty much laughed.

Finally, in desperation, I retreated to my brother's basement with a copy of my resume, a generic cover letter, an old fax machine, and a copy of the Yellow Pages. There I sat for four days faxing a resume to every company where I could imagine myself working. I sent out literally over 1000 resumes. If I had a lot of companies calling me, it seemed logical that I would be able to call the shots on where I wanted to work, instead of trying to choose the best out of one or two opportunities.

At long last I received a call from Darrell Domstad, a division manager with the largest financial planning firm in Canada. I hesitated, expecting this to be more of the same banking business that I wasn't interested in; however, I went to the interview. I virtually challenged him to tell me why I should work for this firm and what could they offer me, not in money, but in a creative and personally rewarding career. His answers excited me about the type of work I could be doing, and I was thrilled when I was offered the position of consultant.

Instead of helping families who were struggling to make ends meet and worrying about bill collectors, I found myself working with families who had hundreds of thousands, even millions to invest and faced other often complex financial problems. Yet in many ways building financial plans was the same as building debt management plans. A family would come in and we would begin by asking them questions — sometimes scores of questions — about their financial situation. Once I had a clear picture of where they stood, I would ask them about their short- and long-term goals to find out where they wanted to be. Within an hour or two I would be helping to determine this family's best strategies to help them reach their goals.

The quest was to get them to where they wanted to go as efficiently as possible using each of the six disciplines of Financial Planning — cash management, retirement planning, investment planning, insurance, and estate planning — all while trying to beat the tax man. I still felt I had to learn the rules of the game first before I could help my clients win the game.

As I met with many of these families, I realized that the problems of very wealthy families were not the least bit different than working-class families who struggled with massive debt. Many of the families with significant incomes of $300K + per year were in worse financial shape than families who earned $35K between both spouses. Of course budgeting was a factor, but not the only factor.

I saw many sides of wealth and debt, from the extreme to the conservative; I was able to see simple behaviors and attitudes towards money. Changing behavior through a few simple disciplined techniques at first was just fun. Then it became painful and I was disheartened to see many families falling into simple pitfalls — particularly young couples who make serious financial mistakes in their twenties, only to be paying for them throughout their thirties. Others were small business owners who built their business through bootstrapping their personal assets, leveraging every asset they could get their hands on.

Others who were so caught up in borrowing money so they could buy things they couldn't afford so they could impress the neighbors they really didn't like anyway.

Some of the mistakes were so simple I was stunned that so many people were unaware that other options were available. Why were these simple techniques not taught in school?

School is great for teaching us how to make money, but horrible at helping us manage it. Why do we demand that our students devote hundreds of hours memorizing useless facts which are forgotten the day after the test? Why was our education system so flawed as to have no training on budgeting, debt management, wealth management, saving, investing, and determining proper insurance planning and even goal setting? The net worth of the average Americans or Canadians isn't positive until age 31; apparently we are expected to learn this stuff from our parents if they knew it, or the school of hard knocks.

My parents, as great as they are, never really taught me about budgeting. This seemed to be something that they would talk about in private. My brothers and I were the beneficiaries of our parents' good planning, but we never got to learn the strategy behind it. I think this is pretty typical of most families.

The more I thought about the troubles many families face, I saw living proof that the number one cause of divorce is related to the strain poor money management brings into the home. In some small way I feel I can make a difference. In this book, I hope to share with you some of the simple truths I've learned from my experience, because if you want to win the game, you've got to know how it's played.

Here goes.

CHAPTER ONE

BUDGETING

YOU CAN'T MANAGE what you can't measure.

I need to start this book by saying I realize that families who are in debt got there for countless different reasons. Not all of these reasons were brought on by themselves. Sometimes in life we find ourselves in situations we just have to deal with, regardless of whether or not we created them. Debt management is more than spending less than you earn. I'm sure if we took a poll on the ways and means of getting in and being in debt, we would have a limitless list that extends from dishonest people who cheated us, to death and disability, to well-intentioned business deals gone bad, to people who are simply fools — and I mean that in the nicest possible way. I may not have seen it all, but I've seen a lot of it.

In this chapter I intend to share some of the most common budgeting mistakes. The purpose of sharing these mistakes is not to identify the idiots in our communities, but to help you learn from the mistakes of others so you do not have to pay the same tuition to the school of hard knocks yourself.

Here's one example of a fool:

In the fall of 1997 I was living in Utah, which incidentally has three times the bankruptcies as the National Average.

One of my appointments was with a young couple. Dave was 22 years old with a high school education and a very high opinion of how he was doing in life. He was a hard working guy and had a great deal going for him. Vanessa, his wife, was a stay home mom who babysat from time to time for extra money. They had a six month old daughter, Hanna.

Dave's father helped him start a company installing hardwood floors. His monthly take-home after taxes was just over $7,000 per month, which for most folks in Utah County is significant, especially considering his age. However, when he came into my office both he and his wife's demeanor quickly went from confidence to a state of confusion. They could not figure out why they were always broke, barely living month to month despite their better than average income. It seemed as though the more money they made, the tighter things seemed to be. They seemed to be running faster and faster on the hamster wheel and never getting ahead — in fact they felt as though they were going backward.

As I began to ask questions, I found out very quickly why cash flow was tight. They, particularly he, are serious impulse buyers without thought or discipline. Here's one example:

The week before I met Dave and Vanessa, Dave was driving his truck home from work. He stopped into the Dodge dealership to find out what was the going rate for a new truck. Without talking with his wife or having any cool-off period, he bought a brand spanking new white Diesel 2500 4X4 truck. It was beautiful. Because of his already high debt servicing ratio (the percent of income already going to service debt) created from other impulse buys, the interest rate on the truck was 12%. He didn't care, if he even noticed; he was dreaming of what this truck would look like in the driveway and how impressed his fellow workers would be.

He asked one of his buddies who worked with him to follow him home in his old truck and he pulled into the driveway with a great big grin on his face. When Vanessa saw the new truck and found out he had bought it without her input, she came unglued. "How on earth could you be so stupid?" she screamed. "Why would you buy something like that without my input? Do you know we are now making payments on your two trucks and my car? Where will this money come from?" She stormed into the bedroom, slammed the door, and locked it.

Of course he felt badly, and as a loving husband he wanted to make things right. He talked her out of the bedroom and that night they went to a Nissan Dealership together and purchased a new Altima for her. So, instead of making three car payments, now they were making <u>four</u> — and incidentally, the Altima was also at 12%.

A few weeks later he was watching television when the mailman arrived. Among the bills were several credit card applications guaranteeing $5000 of credit. Dave rationalized that if all these banks were willing to lend him money that must mean they felt he was strong enough financially to handle another loan. He filled out three of them and returned them. Credit was approved at an average rate of 18% and quickly all three were maxed out.

I'm sure we've heard the analogy of trying to fill a bathtub with the drain open — even if more water is coming in than is going out, it's still going to be hard to fill the tub. Well, this family was draining their financial tub faster than the funds were coming in to replace and build them.

Despite already working near their limits, Dave and

Vanessa felt that if he could just complete one more floor per month or if she could take on one more child to babysit things would come together. Their solution was always running a little faster on the hamster wheel. In the meantime, the pressure was catching up to them and weighing on their marriage.

I believe many families who are seriously in debt are there because of bad budgeting. This brings serious tension into the home. I recently read a survey which indicates that over 87% of families fight about money on a monthly basis. Families in debt because of poor budgeting generally take the following approach:

They work hard all month then bring home the paycheck, pay all necessary bills — mortgage, utilities, insurance, etc. — and whatever is left they throw in the air. The money seems to land where it lands. You know, going out to eat a few more times, catching a couple more movies — until they begin each month at zero, hoping there is not too much month at the end of the money. Then when an emergency arises, they charge it.

By emergency, I don't just mean a major medical crisis. I mean the transmission going, the water heater breaking, the basement flooding, or some aunt in Oregon dying, necessitating a quick flight out at a moment's notice. (NOTE: These things happen to all of us.) But all too often, we don't have any kind of backup plan, and now we have to run a little faster on the hamster wheel to make an additional credit card payment. Over time this single debt turns into several, and we reach a point to where we borrow from Peter to pay Paul and we are running faster and faster on the wheel until we miss a payment and then our finances come crashing down.

Families who are very wealthy take a very different approach. At the very beginning of the month they set money aside. I don't care if it is $10. They then pay their bills and throw the rest up in the air. The main difference is the $10 generates interest and accumulates over time. When the emergencies come in life, they have cash available and consequently, they don't need to charge it. But also, when the opportunities come in life (and NOTE: they happen to all of us), they are in a position to take advantage because they have the cash available. Those opportunities may come in the form of a great rental property; it may be a great deal on a car or a once-in-a-lifetime investment. This small change in behavior makes millionaires. Remember you cannot be an investor until you can first be a saver. Many planners call this strategy, "Paying yourself first."

All growth comes by first looking at the truth. What money is coming in and where is it going?

One of the main reasons budgeting is such a problem is that most families have no budget. Yet I've never seen a family or business become financially successful without one. Good planning makes life much easier. It brings direction and restores peace.

If you are self-employed, you may say that budgeting doesn't apply to you because of the inconsistency of your income. I realize that income derived from different types or streams of employment are inconsistent.

I've always worked on commission and rarely know exactly what my paychecks will be from month to month. I do, however, know exactly what my tagged expenses are and have a pretty good idea of spending habits. I find a spreadsheet works best.

To get an idea of how simple budgeting can be, do this exercise with me.

- Your Monthly Income:_____
- Your Spouse's Monthly Income:_____
- Other Sources of Income_____
- Total Take home after tax

(I like to start with what is actually coming in the door after taxes and other deductions)

Then subtract the following:

- Tithing to the Church or Donations to Charities_____

(notice this is first; I do believe in the law of reciprocity)

- Regular Savings_____
- Mortgage (Principal + interest)_____
- Payments on loans and debts_____
- Groceries_____

(food, cleaning supplies, and all of the little trips throughout the month)

- Clothing_____
- Shelter_____

(rent, repairs, taxes, insurance)

- Utilities_____

(phone, cable, Internet, gas, water, electric, etc.)

- Transportation_____

(gasoline, repairs, insurance, parking, train or bus fares, etc.)

- Insurance_____

(life, disability, health, etc.)

- Direct Medical_____

(dental costs, glasses, prescriptions, etc.)

- Entertainment_____

(movies, dining out, etc.)

- Recreation/ Education_____

(holidays, hobbies, clubs, subscriptions)

- Miscellaneous_____

(donations, dues, child care, alimony, child support, etc.)

- Total Expense_____
- Uncommitted Income_____

When I go through this budgeting exercise with most families, I sometimes sense that they are uncomfortable doing this together for fear the other will finally know where all the income is going. For me, I really don't care. If you spend 80% of your budget on shoes — go for it. I don't think it is right for anyone to tell you how to spend your money; after all, you've earned it. If you choose to live in a dump and drive an $80,000 sports car, that's fine with me. That is a value judgment that you've chosen to make. You've chosen to place value on a car instead of a house. Some choose to drive a clunker and invest their money in their home or clothes or their exotic fish collection. The key is not how you are spending the money, but whether you are comfortable with where the money is going, and whether your plan meets your needs now and in the future.

If you look at where the money is going and are not comfortable with it, then let's make some changes. Feel free to play with the numbers and determine an allocation of resources that meets your needs and makes you happy. Make certain your choices will allow you to enjoy today, and also enjoy your tomorrows. Some people make the mistake of thinking every dime you spend should be practical. Make sure you leave yourself a little room to be unpractical. Remember to have your own personal enjoyment fund. Make the adjustments, measure again next month, and reevaluate. When you are comfortable with where your money is going, you'll have a budget that works for you.

Here are some important things to remember when drawing up a budget.

1. The law of reciprocity — donate first to the church or charities. The prophet Malachi summed it up best when he wrote, "Will a man rob God?, Yet ye have robbed me. But ye say, wherein have we robbed thee; in tithes and offerings. Bring ye all the tithes into the storehouse that there may be meat in mine house, and prove me now herewith, saith the Lord of Hosts, if I will not open you the windows of heaven and pour you out a blessing that there shall not be room enough to receive. And I will rebuke the devourer for your sakes. And your vine shall not cast its fruit before its time in the field." (Malachi 3:8-11) The law of reciprocity is a true principle of money management. Call it Karma, the law of the harvest, or whatever you choose; but when you give you get.

2. When reviewing your budget, go through it from top to bottom. Take a good look at where the money is going. Does it work for you? What needs to stay the same? What needs to be changed? Where can you start? If you're not sure of the exact numbers; ballpark it. Take your best guess. Play with the numbers until they balance. Determine what amount is uncommitted and resolve to set a portion of it aside first from now on. Set it aside where you do not have easy access to it and let it grow. Be like the infomercial guy. Set it and forget it.

3. Recognize budgeting takes discipline. A good plan means nothing unless it is executed. Have confidence in yourself and take action now. Have the discipline to follow your plan.

4. Be reasonable. After I spoke with one young couple about budgeting, the wife was so excited about her new resolve that she insisted her husband turn in every receipt from every item he purchased. She would wait at the front door with her notepad scrutinizing every item he purchased for the day. When he put a quarter into a gumball machine she would snap because there was no receipt and she could not account for every penny.

Start by making a reasonable budget. Don't sweat the small things and feel free to control the budget as tightly or loosely as you feel you need to.

RESULTS: A proper budget gives you control; being in control of your life gives confidence in your future. Good luck with it. THIS WORKS!

CHAPTER TWO

WORK TOGETHER TO FORM A PLAN

WHEN I WAS AT COLLEGE one of my roommates, Frieso, was a real clean freak. Wherever we would go we would find Frieso following behind us with a wet sponge, ready to wipe down every wall and fingerprint we left behind. When I would arrive with my groceries, he would ask if he could put them away — cans and soup packets sorted and stacked by category and alphabetical order. It almost wasn't safe to take a bathroom break after a long session of studying at the kitchen table; you'd return two minutes later to find all of your books closed and stacked neatly on your bed. I chuckle to recall Frieso hovering behind me just waiting to grab my dinner plate so he could clean it.

When friends would come by, they would ask me if Frieso drove me crazy. At first he did. Over time I came to believe that every apartment needs a Frieso. Without Frieso, who knows what our place would have looked like? With him here, all our lives were clean and orderly. I think I've developed a whole new appreciation for order, and have to admit

I've turned into a bit a clean freak because of his influence. When I see many families try to regulate their budget, it is usually with considerable frustration and reluctance to face past mistakes. Usually there is one partner who is very good with money; the other one rarely knows what is in the account and just expects funds to be available whenever he or she feels like going on a spending spree. Having styles that compliment each other are important in any relationship.

I met an older family in Central California where the husband could be referred to as the worst kind of miser. He refused to spend a dime on anything. If the children had to go without shoes, so be it. He lived through the Depression and the mandate was to save 30% of income regardless.

In doing this they made extreme sacrifices. Rarely did they treat their children; the family never took a vacation, and they always wore hand-me-downs as the militant father had to have a tight rein on the expenses.

I met them during their retiring years; they had piles of money in the bank, poor health, and a lifetime of regrets for things they were never able to enjoy.

On the other side of the scale, there is another couple I met in Dallas. They were in their retiring years and didn't have any savings whatsoever. Lucy would call me periodically to tell me what an idiot she thought her husband was. She felt that her duty in life was to get him to hold back and his duty was to drive her nuts by making stupid purchases. One of the main things that bothered her was when he spent large sums of money on things that weren't tangible — ski trips, vacations and expensive dinners. Lucy felt she and her husband were never on the same page when it came to life's goals.

Despite her ridicule, however, she was a worse spender

than he was. She seemed to be forever keeping score; if he spent his money foolishly, so would she. If he went skiing, she'd buy a new dress. Instead of reeling each other in, the act of spending money was a way of ticking each other off. Consequently, in their retiring years they were forced to turn to their children for financial aid, as their poor decisions and lack of savings finally caught up with them.

My wife made an interesting point to me last night: there needs to be continual communication when it comes to goals and budget. It's not a one-time thing. Goals should be clearly negotiated between couples, renegotiated whenever necessary, and both partners should work towards a balanced budget and plan.

One of the greatest things about Frieso was the way his desires complimented the other five of us. The worst situation you can have is two extreme spenders or two extreme tightwads. Life is too short; balance is the key. Enjoy your todays and plan to enjoy your tomorrows.

Now I imagine the one who is most thrifty in your relationship is the one who purchased this book. He or she is probably also the one who holds the purse strings or is the manager of the money. If this is you, entice your partner to read the book as well, and work together on setting goals. Invite a financial planner to help you set long and short term goals; sometimes your partner needs to hear it from a third party. If you can't talk some sense into your partner, perhaps the planner can! The planner can undoubtedly share a couple of personal experiences about their own Daves and Vanessas.

I cannot stress enough the value of sitting together and discussing goals. Imagine for a moment you and your spouse stopped by the office of a travel agent to book a trip. The travel agent would have to ask questions:

1. Where do you plan to go?
2. When do you plan to leave?
3. How long do you plan to stay there?
4. What can you afford to spend on the vacation?
5. Why is this trip important? What is it about that area that appeals to you and what other areas could potentially offer the same value at a better price?

By setting a destination and a deadline for the management of your finances, we are progressing together to get you any where you want to go — and I'm not just talking about a holiday. We are making it possible for you to not only manage your money but your entire life.

CHAPTER THREE

CONSOLIDATION AND COMPRESSION

WHEN I FIRST MET WITH DAVE AND VANESSA, they told me that they had recently finished a consolidation loan. This is how they went about it. At the time Dave had three credit cards with interest rates at 18%, and between the three he had a balance of around $10,000. While watching television he saw a commercial offering a package in which all loans could be "consolidated into one payment." Dave was thrilled. What a headache to try to keep up with three payments when one payment would do the trick! He made the call and found out his new rate would be 36%. Dave did the math and concluded that one 36% card was better than three 18's, so he transferred the three balances to one card.

So Dave and Vanessa found themselves paying just over $300 per month interest on the loan. I remember the evening distinctly. Neither Dave nor Vanessa really understood interest, and they simply didn't get the concept of what the difference was. I explained to them that interest was the cost of borrowing the money. If the interest rate is high — 36%

is very high — you are being charged more to borrow the money than as if the interest rate was low. After going around and around for 45 minutes I couldn't get through to Dave or Vanessa why lower interest rates were preferable to higher ones. I used every analogy I could think of; even simple math wouldn't work. If they owed $10,000 at 36% they would be paying $3,600 in interest every year ($10,000 X .36); if they owed $10,000 at 6% they would only pay $600 ($10,000 X .06) a year. What would they rather pay to have the same benefit of borrowing $10,000? After two hours I told Dave to trust me and I would do it for them. I'm convinced to this day if I were to hold three one dollar bills in my left hand and a one hundred dollar bill in my right and ask Dave to pick which one he'd rather keep, Dave would choose the three one dollar bills because there are more of them.

A consolidation or compression loan is a new loan whose overall credit limit is large enough to encompass all other high-interest debts you may have, and which carries a lower rate of interest than you had been paying before. You may not qualify for a loan big enough to absorb all your debts, but if the bank is willing lend you a smaller amount, place the highest interest debts within this loan first. The goal is to bring down the average interest rates as much as possible.

For example, if your total debt payments were $450 per month with the higher interest rates, we could lower the monthly payment to $250 just by consolidating these debts in a loan with lower interest. Because of the lower interest rate, $200 drops off the payment you are required to make. The key with a consolidation loan, however, is to continue making the $450 payment. Why on earth would you do that? Because that additional $200 now goes towards the principal, not the interest, and you will pay off the loan more quickly. If $450 is more than you can afford, drop down the payment slightly — perhaps to $400 — but whatever you do don't drop the payment all the way to $250. By keeping the payments higher, the additional $200 is chopping down the principal and paying off the loan at a very accelerated rate.

There are a couple of potential pitfalls to this strategy. Once your credit card debt has been compressed into one lower interest loan, the credit card balances are at zero. This can be a very dangerous situation for someone with little discipline, especially if they've been in the habit of using their credit cards for every little purchase. Quickly, those credit card balances begin to creep up again because the consumer has not changed his spending habits, and in no time the cards are maxed out. This time, however, our consumer has two payments: the $250 from his recent consolidation, and $450 for his newly maxed out credit cards. The consolidation just bought enough time to rack the credit cards up again. This time the bank sees that a very high percent of income is going to service the debt and they are not too excited about issuing another consolidation. The total amount debt has soared to include both the consolidation and new credit card debt, and the amount our consumer is flushing away in interest payments has grown rather than diminished.

Do yourself a big favor. If you even suspect for a moment you lack the discipline to control credit card spending, choose one card and ask your bank to reduce your credit limit to something that can easily be paid in full every month. Then cut the rest of your cards up! Get rid of them! Chop them up and burn them! Almost everyone needs one credit card in today's world — to reserve hotel rooms, rent a car, or make purchases on the Internet. But for the life of me I can't see a reason to have more than one personal card. Remember the old adage: is if it cannot be paid off in a month and it isn't life threatening — put it away. Even better yet, get a Visa or MasterCard check card that automatically withdrawals funds from your checking account. If you don't have the money for the purchase in the account, no transaction can occur.

Never forget the cost of borrowing money; it is sobering. J. Reuben Clark says, "Interest never sleeps nor sickens nor dies; it never goes to the hospital; it works on Sundays and holidays; it never takes a vacation; it never visits nor travels; it takes no pleasure; it is never laid off work nor discharged from employment; it never works on reduced hours. Once in debt, interest is your companion every minute of the day and night; you cannot shun it or slip away from it; you cannot dismiss it; it yield neither to entreaties, demands, or orders, and whenever you get in its way or cross its course or fail to meet its demands, it crushes you." That damn interest eats you alive; avoid it like the plague or it will steal your financial future.

One of the big problems I have with American taxation system is that interest is tax deductible on a mortgage. This is a huge mistake. I've met families who've lived in their home for 28 years with less than $3,000 in equity. Every couple of years when credit card and car payments begin to accumulate, they spend between $2,500 and $3,000 to refinance their mortgage so they can maximize their beloved interest deduction. The key is to pay off your mortgage, get rid of debt, and have a mortgage-free home, not to maximize debt to encourage a tax deduction!

Families should not be rewarded in any way to carry debt. Surely the government can eliminate the deduction and creatively find a way to give it to us elsewhere. They justify pulling your home into your estate and taxing it by claiming you received a deduction for it. My feeling is if they need the estate tax, keep it in place; however, don't reward people for keeping any level of debt. Why would we give a big benefit to those carrying big mortgages and penalize the renters who can't qualify for the deduction? I can't see the logic in it.

I get sick to my stomach hearing Financial Planners recommend to their clients to take on more debt, buy a bigger home so they can be eligible for bigger deductions. Bigger homes and bigger mortgages also bring bigger property taxes, and bigger utilities, and bigger maintenance bills. Why would we recommend strategies that are contrary to logic? Pay off your homes and eliminate your debt.

In a declining interest rate environment, many have jumped on the refinancing bandwagon. The rule of thumb is to not refinance your home for any reason unless you can save a full two percentage points. If you're saving at least 2 full percentage points and plan on living in the home long term, then good for you — refinance. Determine how long you've got to live in the home to recoup the cost of the refinancing. If you don't know how to do this, ask your loan officer to determine how long it will take to break even based on the new refinance charges you are adding to the loan. Refinancing your home can be tempting especially when there is equity and considerable other debt. My recommendation is to use judgment. Count the costs and only pull the trigger if there are considerable savings after all refinancing costs have been tallied. Then chart a course to ensure you'll never need to pull that trigger again. Not unless you can save at least another 2%.

When looking at your debt load to determine if a consolidation is in your best interest, the first place a homeowner should look is the home. Your home is a secured asset, and financial institutions lend money at the lowest rates on secured assets.

Put yourself in the position of the bank. If you were lending money to someone, one of the main things you would look for is collateral. If this person defaults on the loan, what can you take to get your money back? A secured asset like a home is good because if the borrower doesn't pay, the bank can take something that should hold its value and thus get their money back. This sounds ominous, but makes you a good candidate for consolidation.

On a secured debt the first ratio we look at is loan to value. If the value of the home were $200,000 and the existing mortgage was $100,000, the loan to value ratio would be calculated ($100,000/$200,000) giving us 50%. A conventional loan will generally lend lend as high as 75% LTV (Loan to Value) on a property. So in this case we have $50,000 of room for a consolidation.

The next question would be, "What would it cost to consolidate?" Generally when consolidating a debt into a home loan we can get the lowest rates, but also we have higher costs to close the loan. If we took a separate line of credit secured by the home, the rate would be higher but the cost to close would be lower. Let's weigh the numbers both ways and see what would be better. You don't have to be a mathematician; if you're not confident in running the numbers, have your financial planner do it and advise you. The key is to get the closing costs and rates for both options and then run them against each other. Ten minutes spent here could save you tens of thousands.

Generally the best way to look at a consolidation is first to look at rolling debt into a secured loan against an asset like a home. The best rates are generally against the first mortgage which would be conventional (less the 75% LTV); the next most desirable solution would be a secured second mortgage followed by a higher rate unconventional loan, a loan using any type of security, and finally an unsecured loans based on income. Start at the top and work your way down. There are always exceptions to these rules if there are introductory rates, closing cost deals, or special circumstances, but generally these rules hold true.

I threw a lot of numbers, formulas, ratios, and concepts at you in this chapter. You may think that if you just pay your bills you'll never have to worry about any of these things, but there you'd be wrong. If you faithfully pay the minimum payment on your credit card bill and continue to use the card, you will never get out of debt. If you consolidate your bills to make your payments more affordable, you may actually wind up paying (and owing) more than you did to begin with. If you refinance your home for the same term every time you want a little extra cash, you will never pay off your house. Watch the numbers — run them often — and understand what you're doing! This is why you need a financial planner you trust.

CHAPTER FOUR

DEBT STACKING

WHILE DOING DEBT MANAGEMENT IN UTAH, I was surprised to find myself on an appointment to one of the wealthiest areas of the state. I pulled my Mazda up to a million dollar home and walked inside to meet the family. I always prefer to meet with both spouses so I can make sure they are both on the same page, especially when it comes to goals (remember Chapter 2). However, when I arrived I found that Donna, the wife, was gone. I should have rescheduled the appointment, but the day was beautiful and Ted invited me to join him on their gorgeous veranda.

Ted began to talk, and I listened. He began by telling me that he's had a problem with budgeting all his life and up until now he'd never seen a need for it. His income was well in the $450K range. He had come from money and had always been around and made good money. However, as Ted was approaching retirement, he'd found himself in an uncomfortable situation; he had nothing.

As I began to gather information, we first reviewed the mortgage. Although Ted and Donna had lived in the home for fifteen years, there was only 30K in equity, which made

JAMIE D. VERMEEREN CFP FMA

for one large mortgage and an even bigger monthly mortgage payment — in excess of $10,000 per month. Next we went to lines of credit; they had four, all maxed out, and totaling just under $180,000. We then went to outstanding credit accounts, the hot tub payment, dental bills, Jet Ski payments, snowmobile payments, in addition to credit cards debt alone totaling an additional $120K. The list continued. Debt management consultants call this being broke at a higher level, and Ted and Donna were. The bottom line is you're still living month to month praying you don't get sick or the large house of cards will come crashing down quickly.

Now Ted and Donna weren't without assets. They had a vintage convertible Mercedes Benz and hundreds of thousands of dollars of jewelry and trinkets that they'd collected from traveling all around the world. They seemed to have plenty of antiques and other assets that weren't liquid and assured me they couldn't bear to lose their jewelry and antique trinkets.

They hadn't defaulted on any loans yet, but were (barely) hanging on. With an income that was still strong, they wanted to give debt management a try in lieu of bankruptcy. I agreed. Why should the taxpayers eat their debt; they made it, and with the right planning they were capable of getting out! I also couldn't bear to see them part with all of their life's collections.

We first thought we'd look at a consolidation option to try to lower the high interest credit cards and other consumer debt as their credit was still in good shape. I figured with the reduction in payments we could free up some cash flow and apply more of the new found cash to principal.

Unfortunately, turned out Ted and Donna had some credit

issues in the past and the bank wasn't keen on extending any more loans. We tried a few other lenders to no avail. After checking out several lenders we determined consolidation was a weak option. So we took a serious look at debt stacking. This is how it works:

The best way to execute this strategy is on a spreadsheet--excel works great. At the top of each column write the name of the debt with interest rate behind it and just beneath it the minimum payment; like so:

Furniture	Hot Tub	VISA	DENTAL	PLOC
28%	22%	18%	12%	9%
Payments	Payments	Payments	Payments	Payments
$100	$100	$100	$100	$100
$100	$100	$100	$100	$100
$100	$100	$100	$100	$100
$100 ⟶	$100	$100	$100	$100
Paid OFF	$200	$100	$100	$100
EUPHORIA!!!	$200	$100	$100	$100
	$200	$100	$100	$100
	$200	$100	$100	$100
	Paid OFF	$300	$100	$100
	6 months of	$300	$100	$100
	Interest	$300	$100	$100
	Saved	$300	$100	$100
	EUPHORIA!!!	$300	$100	$100
		$300	$100	$100
		Paid OFF	$400	$100
		18 months of	$400	$100
		Interest	$400	$100
		Saved	$400	$100
		EUPHORIA!!!	$400	$100
			$400	$100
			$400	$100
			$400	$100
			Paid OFF	$500
			24 months of	$500
			Interest	$500
			Saved	$500
			EUPHORIA!!!	$500
				$500
				$500
				Paid OFF
				35 months of
				Interest
				Saved
				EUPHORIA!!!

Step ONE: In the above list I've placed the highest interest rate debt — in this case, the furniture — in the far left column, placed the debt with the next highest interest rate in the column next to it, and so on in descending order from left to right.

Step TWO: Make minimum payments on all debts except the one at the far left. The big error most families make is when they have a little extra cash and throw an extra $20-30 dollars on each debt. Soon they get discouraged as they feel that these extra payments make little difference (and they're right). Let's make some changes. If you find you have any additional cash after making your required payments, put all of it toward the payment in the far left position. When all extra payments are going to one debt, the principal erodes much faster. When the furniture is finally paid off, we are in a state of euphoria!!! We see our extra effort is making a difference.

Without too much celebrating, we reroute the cash we used to have to pay toward the furniture store payment to the hot tub payment, which now becomes the unpaid debt in the furthest left position. Of course, any extra cash goes toward the hot tub payment as well. The full amount of this extra cash payment goes to principal. Chopping down principal is the only way to erode debt, and now we are doing it at an accelerated rate. When the hot tub is done (6 months ahead of schedule), we increase our rate of acceleration by moving the cash that was used for the furniture payment and the hot tub payment and roll it to the Visa. Keep doing this for a while and you'll see we've saved 24 months of interest payments. The total amount we are paying every month has not changed. It has remained identical ever since we were paying on the furniture and the hot tub.

We are now making headway. Each time we get rid of a debt we feel ourselves moving closer to our goal of being debt free, and the euphoria grows. We find ourselves budgeting better and rerouting more and more towards paying off debt. Each time we roll over the cash from the previous debt we increase the rate of acceleration.

This strategy WORKS, but it takes discipline — a lot of it. Paying off the furniture is a great thing. We've just freed up $100 per month in cash flow. But most families feel that $100 burning a hole in their pocket, and they've got to spend it. Heaven knows our wish lists are long. Don't spend that money! Reroute and reroute that money to the next debt before you get used to spending it — chop away at that principal until the very last debt is gone.

The hardest part about this strategy is discipline. When you see extra cash available, allocate it immediately. Don't plan on enjoying it for a few months first — it will evaporate in the budget and you'll never see it again. Or worse yet, in a moment of weakness you or your spouse will come up with a new monthly payment to impress the neighbors and you're back to square one. I've said it before and I'll say it again — we get into debt to buy things we cannot afford to impress the neighbors we really don't like anyways. Why fall into that trap? Pay off, reroute, and accelerate!

CHAPTER FIVE

UNDERSTANDING YOUR CREDIT

WHEN I WAS IN COLLEGE, one of my accounting professors told me; "Whatever you do in this life, protect your credit." At the time I didn't think much of it. After all, at that point I basically had no credit; I had no assets, no income, no liabilities and at the time no job. The only loan I'd ever had was for a car I bought in high school. Since I had no credit, my mom and dad cosigned a $5000 loan for an 85 Oldsmobile Firenza, and I paid for it by bagging groceries at the Safeway.

Every week I made payments and after two years she was mine. What a money pit that car was. It seemed as though the only reason I worked was so I could afford the gas, insurance, payment and constant repair bills. As a teenager it was the best thing for me. I had to work evenings and weekends to have and maintain that car; this kept me broke and the work kept me too busy to get into trouble. In short, it was a great way to teach me responsibility.

When I was sixteen I made some dumb decisions and took my car onto an outdoor hockey rink to spin donuts in an effort to impress the girls. That episode cost me approximately $600. Later I blew the engine while on a ski trip with friends — that expense was $1600. When I look back at the mistakes I made, I'm grateful for them. Those mistakes taught me accountability for my actions. Luckily I was blessed to have parents who didn't bail me out and wanted me to learn expensive lessons in my youth instead of in my thirties. I soon recognized the consequences of foolish actions and vowed to make better choices in the future. I had to learn to value and protect things. Learning from the school of hard knocks can take time, hard work and patience.

When it comes to maintaining good credit, my professor was right; loans are easier to get, interest rates are better, and terms are more favorable if your credit is good. How do we build good credit, and how do we destroy it?

Almost all lenders in the United States make all lending decisions based on your FICO score. The word FICO means Fair Isaac Company, this is the name of the company who first got the idea to record and track credit, then condense all credit information to come up with a number to rank your credit history. This score is typically a number between zero and 800. A number over 640 is considered good — or an A quality credit. Ratings, like bonds, can be rated up to AAAA all the way down to B, C, and D. In the United States three major credit bureaus gather credit information and report that information using the FICO system: Equifax, TransUnion, and Experian.

The first way to have a weak grade is to have no credit at all. This problem usually affects people in their younger years who have no history of payments going through their name — in other words, no track record. This can also be an issue with couples who have everything in the name of one spouse, failing to include the other spouse on credit applications, mortgages, utility bills, and the like. This is a really bad idea; should they ever divorce, or if the one with everything in his or her name dies, the spouse with no credit history will be very hard pressed to get a loan with favorable terms.

What the lender wants to see is a track record of consistency. They want to see that you have undertaken a financial obligation, have a track record of making payments, and are good at paying loans off or a least being consistent with monthly bills.

The easiest way to do this is to get a small credit card from your bank. A bank will usually give a credit line of $500 if you have a pulse and an income. Use it for something simple like putting gas on it and pay it off monthly. The bank will see a history and your credit will begin to develop very quickly. Over the course of two years going from no credit to excellent credit is easy.

The main way FICO points are deducted is if payments arrive late. Marks are deducted for 30, 60, 90 and 120 days late and rest assured it is easier to lose points that to acquire them. So whatever you do make your payment on time. A rule of thumb with credit cards is — if you can't afford to pay it off that month — then don't put it on. Now I understand that emergencies come and exceptions have to be made. Just use good judgment. If you miss one bill for 120 days, you lose points at the 30 day mark, the 60 day mark, the 90 and 120 day mark. Thus if you have one bill that you miss, the damage created can really hurt.

The next way you lose points is the number of times your credit gets checked. Usually you lose 2-3 points for each occurrence. If there are lots and lots of creditors checking your credit, this is a great big, red flag for the lender. They want to know why. Sometimes shopping around for a great interest rate can do more harm than good if it causes many lenders to run a credit check. However, no one can check your credit rating without your social security number and your signature. When shopping around, keep this in mind. There should never be a reason to have more than five different companies check your credit.

With any rule there are exceptions. Suppose you've always been good at making payments. Then you have a sickness, disability, or divorce and payments get messy for a while. Over time you get back on track. The bad credit on your report will take years to come off — usually seven. When you apply for a loan and have this type of blemish, we can generally clear them up quite easily. We start by writing a letter to the lending institution explaining that this was an isolated incident. The condition which caused this incident no longer exists; this blemish is not likely to ever repeat. Based on previous credit history, before the blemish, the lender now can use their discretion to determine if they want to lend the funds. My experience has shown that if the incident can be explained and the situation was reasonable considering the circumstances in most cases you'll get the loan at a reasonable rate.

You might be quite surprised to see how much detail is on your credit report. Credit reports have your name, address, birth date, and consumer alert which determine if anyone has tried to be fraudulent with your credit. Your credit report will show if collections have ever come against you and the collections generally fall into three areas depending upon what the lender has done:

1. You have made an arrangement with the lender to pay back the loan or modify the payments.
2. There has been a voluntary or involuntary repossession of assets
3. The loan has gone to collections or the lender has written it off

Obviously no lender will be excited about lending you more money until these issues have been resolved. If they do grudgingly give you a loan, they will add a premium in the interest rate to compensate them for taking a higher risk.

Your credit report will also include a file number, dates of last activity (the last time credit was applied for), where you work, your title at work and even former employers.

The last two sections are also very important:
1. Who is making inquires on your credit?
2. What debt are you currently holding?

No single factor tells the whole story; but together they paint a pretty clear picture of past history.

As important as credit is, it is not everything. Your credit score is just one of the factors that go into determining if you get the loan or not. Other factors include your ability to service the debt. In other words — will you have the cash to make the payments? If cash flow is weak, the lender may also lend money based on the collateral of borrower. For example, if there is no cash flow, but you own property, you can secure the loan against the property using it as collateral for the loan.

At the end of the day all credit boils down to the four C's.

CHARACTER

This is a big one. When an institution reviews character they want to determine how you've done in the past when it comes to paying off debts and loans. What does history tell us? How many times have you been late over 30, 60, or 90 days? Is there an explanation? Was it an isolated incident or a regular occurrence? Why should an institution lend its resources and at what risk? Banks or any institution are interested in one big thing — covering their assets. They'll cover themselves by making certain you're a good bet. If they believe that you are a higher risk, they will add what is called a risk premium. This usually is a couple of percentage points added to the interest rate to compensate the bank for taking a gamble on you. The higher the gamble — the higher the risk premium.

On the other hand, if you've proven to have good character by honoring the agreements of your previous loans in the past, you will be entitled to better rates and more favorable terms.

CAPACITY

The next question a lender asks is capacity to pay back the loan. There are a couple of ratios used to calculate if the person has the capacity to take the loan. The first ratio is the Total Debt Servicing ratio. Add your annual mortgage payments (or rent) + property taxes + heating costs + plus 50% of condo fees + all debt payments and divide it by your annual gross family income. This number should be under 40%. This is the ratio used most often.

If there are credit accounts open with no balances on them, typically a lending institution will calculate the Total Debt Service Ratio as though those accounts were maxed out and you were paying on them monthly, or they will ask you to

GET YOURSELF OUT OF DEBT NOW!

close the account. This gives them reassurance that they are controlling their risk.

The next means for determining capacity is Gross Debt Servicing Ratio. This is a little easier. To calculate it, add your annual mortgage (or rent) + property taxes +heating + 50% of condo fees, all divided by Gross Annual Income. This number should always come in below 32%.

When these numbers climb higher than the benchmark, a risk rating will be applied to the rate. If we don't want the higher rate we will either need to show more income or reduce current debt before applying for the loan. Self-employed people often struggle with this one. They are always fighting to show a very small income to the taxman while trying to show a big income to the lender.

CAPITAL

Banks want to see collateral, and they give preferred rates to those with it. So much so that at times we shout at them and say if I had all of the collateral you're asking for I wouldn't need the loan! In addition to good character and capacity, lenders love to see that a loan is secured by something you own. This guarantees that they'll get their money bank, even if you default. The more capital we build the better. This is why savings should always be a crucial component to any plan.

CREDIT RATING

As far as I'm concerned Credit Rating and Character are one in the same. Your credit report shows what your character has been like over the past seven years. You are then assigned a ranking based on what your credit looks like. Checking your credit is very easy and can be done for a very nominal fee, usually under $15.

Checking your credit is important and should be reviewed. While living in Utah. I decided to pull my credit. To my surprise there was a lender on my credit report I'd never heard of, and they were showing that I was 30 days late on a payment for $60. I was understandably concerned and called my credit bureau to find out what this was. They suggested I call the lender, which I did. Upon checking their records they agreed that we'd never done business together. I asked them to write a letter stating that we had not done business before and requested that they remove this mistake from my credit report. They agreed and the error was fixed.

I suggest you that you should have your credit pulled — not often, but every few years — to make certain there are no errors. I wonder how many loans are denied or given a lower rating that they should have based on flaws in the credit report; it's worth checking out.

For those who've made mistakes in the past, repent and do better. Start by:
1. Spending less than you make — make the budget balance.
2. Call creditors and work with them to create a repayment plan.
3. Keep track of all credit card purchases.
4. Don't take any crap! The laws are on your side. Debtors cannot legally call you before 8 am or after 9 pm; they cannot harass your family or friends; they cannot garnish your wages without legal action. When debtors cross the line, take action by calling the Federal Trade Commission at 1-877-FTC-HELP.

But remember, it's a lot easier to create good credit from the outset than to fix a long history of bad credit. Protect your credit — it's dollars in the bank!

CHAPTER SIX

DETERMINING VALUE

WHEN I WAS NINE OR TEN YEARS OLD, all the kids in our neighborhood rode BMX bikes. It's funny how important the bikes were to us. We would pedal our way to a nearby dirt track and practice taking jumps for hours on end. One day in particular, one of the boys was showing off the latest bike his parents just got him — a PK Ripper. Each of us took turns showing off our own bike and one-upping each other on how much our folks spent on it. I still remember my Kuwahara was $219. There was a dumb sort of pride knowing that it cost a lot. Even if our parents had purchased the exact same item, if there was one that cost more, somehow it was better — but we weren't sure why. Privately we were all cheap and had empty wallets; but to our friends, we wanted to be seen as having it all.

In my twenties, my college friends thought a little differently. None of us bragged about how much we paid. We bragged about the exact opposite — how little we paid and who got the most for the least. At a store that sold crate-damaged goods, I purchased a brand new Tommy Hilfiger shirt for $3 — and later spotted the exact same shirt in the mall for

$75. The idea of paying more for the same thing seemed nothing short of stupid.

Make no mistake, quality often does have a price that is worth paying for; but it should still be a better price than the guy across the street is selling it for.

There can be great discrepancies from one store to another when it comes to price and that's okay. There are many factors that add to the value of the purchase that are worth paying for: the service, warranty, resale value, quality of workmanship, and the list goes on. Our job as consumers is to get most overall value for our dollar — anything less is contrary to the spirit of capitalism.

One of my friends took this to the extreme. When he and his wife went grocery shopping, they would check virtually every newspaper to determine where the very best grocery deals were. Then they would spend the better part of two days visiting each of the stores to save a nickel. If they could save 10 cents on a can of peas they would travel to the moon and back.

Yet this same guy walked into only one auto dealership and purchased a used Toyota Corolla, paying full sticker price with no negotiation. I think it was his first semi-major purchase and he was intimidated by the process. It seems so ironic that a guy who would obsess for two days over peas couldn't compare prices at two or three different auto dealerships.

Time is money. When considering the number of hours wasted and gas money spent, I don't image the ten cents saved on the can of peas went as far as he'd hoped. If you are going to drive around and spend considerable amount of time shopping make sure your savings are worth it.

What my wife and I have done is set a limit. Whenever we

expect to spend over $100, we get three prices from three different stores. We do this with furniture, vacations, blenders, cameras, televisions — you name it. Even when purchasing more expensive clothing, we don't buy until we are certain we've got a good deal, and we cross-reference our purchase with at least three vendors. On larger items we plan on owning for a while — vehicles or homes, for example — we often check four or five different vendors.

One of the wealthiest people I've ever met often shops for months and puts together spreadsheets to make certain he's getting the very best for the very least. The more expensive his purchase, the more effort he puts in to make sure he's negotiated the very best deal for himself or his company. His research includes references, warranty reviews, service comparisons, ongoing maintenance costs, depreciation, location, selection — the works.

Price is important, but it is only one factor when determining which product or service is the best. Warranties are also a big deal; if the company won't stand behind their product, I want to know why. As I write this, I've been in the market to buy a truck for about a year. I was getting pretty serious about either a Chevy, Ford, Dodge, or Toyota. While watching a documentary on the suspension problems of Ford — and all companies have had problems, Ford is not alone in that respect — I was surprised to see that they were shirking their duty by not correcting the problem at their expense, forcing customers whose trucks were under warranty to foot the bill. I was turned off and this eliminated one choice for me.

I'd purchased a Chevy Venture Van for my wife Stacy a couple of year earlier and before the vehicle had reached 1000 clicks, I was back in with several minor problems. The motor on the windshield wipers burnt out at 800; the power windows broke at 900; and the ventilation system fell apart at 950. I appreciated that Chevy would make the repairs at no cost to me; but I felt that wasn't the issue. They wasted a great deal of my time with a faulty product, leaving me convinced their quality control has a great deal to be desired. The dealer kept joking that this vehicle must have been built on a Friday afternoon. The joke wasn't all that funny, considering the cash I'd just dropped on a brand new vehicle. I was also very concerned that when this product came off warranty I might be stuck with a lemon. Despite having been a Chevy guy all my life, I'm just not sure I want to go through the frustration of owning a Chevy again. It comes as no surprise to me their market share is dropping like a rock.

So now I was down to two: the Dodge and the Toyota. I had to do a double check on what would serve me best and why. I liked both products and both had strong reputations of quality.

I was pleased with the quality and loved the power of the Dodge 5.7 liter Hemi; but the more I thought about it, I decided the power (and corresponding fuel costs) was really more than what I needed. I determined that the Toyota's smaller V8, the company's positive reputation, and the four doors for the family meant that was the right truck for me. My wife and I decided to wait for the new 2005 models to arrive and asked the sales rep at the dealership closest to my home to call me as soon as they came in. She took my name and number and promised she would. I waited.

While driving home from work I saw the new Tundras and figured I would wait for the phone call from this sales rep as I felt she should get first crack at the sale. I never heard

58

from her. I called the dealership a couple of weeks later and asked to speak to a new vehicle sales rep. After waiting for about fifteen minutes on the phone I got a salesperson named Jim. I asked Jim to tell me the models and pricing of a new Tundra. He assured me he would call me back as he was busy and took my number, Again, I never heard from him. I decided, even if the vehicle cost more elsewhere, service is worth paying for. I also felt strongly that if this was the service I was getting before I made the purchase; where would they be down the road when I really needed them? I couldn't with a clear conscience give them my business --they didn't deserve it.

I drove past that dealership, and walked into Heninger Toyota wearing an old pair of jeans and a winter coat. After looking for a couple of minutes; I was greeted by the sales manager, Dan Collard. He took the time to determine what I wanted and helped to show me some good alternatives.

I had shopped the market and knew what a good price would be. Because Dan took the time to listen, he recommended that I consider a model from the previous year as they were blowing out at lower prices, and there were two left in Alberta that would meet my needs. I knew I had to strike fast and put a deposit on the vehicle that day.

Dan called me the next day and told me that the 2004 I had been promised was in an accident and the dealership was unable to get it. However, he offered me a 2005 at the same price. Honoring your word and following through with a promise is good business and I've recommended at least four additional sales to them over the next two months.

I'm a firm believer that once you know what you need, know the market, and are certain you've got a good deal you can afford — strike. But make sure you've done your homework first! Taking time to do your homework does a couple of things: it gives you a cooling-off period to ensure that you are making the purchase for the right reasons, and it helps you make the best decision when it comes to price, quality, warranty, and all the other factors that go into making an informed choice.

Some companies are notorious for pressuring you to make decisions before any evaluation period is possible. Timeshare companies are a prime example. You must make the purchase NOW! There is no time for research; there is no time to do your homework. Their job is to get you all fired up so you'll sign on the dotted line. They encourage you to make an uninformed decision based on hype and emotion instead of logic and reasoning. Don't fall for this! Know your market and always compare three alternatives.

By the way, did you know you can purchase a timeshare for roughly 1/3 the price if you buy it on the Internet? Unfortunately, timeshare salespeople won't tell you that.

How do you make an informed decision? Here are a few suggestions.

1. Read, read, and read. Check product reviews in magazines such as *Car and Driver* or *Consumer Reports*. Chart the strengths and weaknesses of products that interest you.

2. Ask advice from trusted friends.

3. Ask for references.

4. Talk to at least three vendors before making your decision. If you feel the pressure is too thick, walk out and don't go back. If the deal were that good, the salesperson wouldn't have to be so aggressive.

Finally, make sure that your purchases are made when you are in a rational frame of mind. My wife has a friend that has experienced the ups and downs of depression. When her depression hits, it stays for several days at a time and she has a hard time pulling herself out. As a means of coping, she feels that if she can treat herself to something nice she it will help her to feel better.

While I am not a psychologist and know little about psychology, I do understand the story of Pavlov and his dogs. Just before he would bring the dogs food, Pavlov would ring a bell. The dogs became conditioned to understand that when the bell rang, the food would arrive shortly. Hence, they would begin to salivate.

After a while, Pavlov would ring the bell and not bring food, yet the dogs would salivate anyway. The message is that some conditioned responses become extremely ingrained within us — we salivate on cue and don't know why.

This has many applications to our daily lives. For example, if a parent yells at their child and feels guilty for their overreaction, they will help their child feel better using a variety of techniques. The parent may buy the child something or feed them a special treat. As humans we associate "feeling better" to patterns our parents help ingrain in us — just like Pavlov and his dogs.

Make no mistake, these conditioned patterns produce a result that is difficult to change. The truth is, buying something does not make one feel better — it is temporary and hollow. Because it is hollow, it does not satisfy. The pattern of depression continues as one grows deeper in debt.

If you've fallen into a cycle of depression and are purchasing items on credit to make yourself feel better, get credit

JAMIE D. VERMEEREN CFP FMA

counseling immediately. In the United States there are two main networks of credit counseling agencies — the National Foundation for Credit Counseling and the Association of Independent Consumer Credit Counseling Agencies. These agencies will tell you where to get the needed help to fix the immediate problems, set up a long term solution, and get on the path to a prosperous future.

CHAPTER SEVEN

MAXIMIZING VALUE

WE ALL WANT THE SAME THING — the most value for our dollar — because we only have so many of them. Even Donald Trump has a scarcity of dollars. In economics the amount of satisfaction we get for something is defined as its utility. If we strapped a "utility meter" to our arm it would measure the amount of satisfaction we receive by making a purchase — regardless of whether it is a good or service. Let's say our "utility meter" measures satisfaction on a scale of 1-10. 1 would bring little satisfaction and 10 we would be bouncing off the ceiling. The degrees on our scale are called utils. It tells us how much utility or value we get from purchasing one good over another.

For example: You and I go out to eat. We have a great filling meal and the waiter comes by with a dessert menu. We check our "utility meter" to ask ourselves whether we would get more value out of buying a dessert or more value out of having the money in our pocket as we walk out the door?

Another example: My favorite food is cookies, and I have a big plate of them in front of me. The first cookie I eat brings a util value of 8 — it was great! The second cookie scores a 6 —

still pretty good. The third cookie only rates a 3 (I've had my fill), the fourth cookie a 1 (still okay but getting worse), and the 5th cookie starts to gross me out and brings a negative 2 satisfaction. By my third cookie my utility meter is telling me a glass of milk would rank about 6. In other words, as much as I like cookies, once I've enjoyed the initial satisfaction, the satisfaction level goes down. I would prefer a glass of milk to another cookie.

Determining value is very difficult, especially considering we all value different things for different reasons. Most of us purchase things that tell ourselves or others who we really are or who we would like to be. We are all motivated by four things:

1. Our image of ourselves
2. Our standing or position within a social group or community
3. Our image of ourselves financially
4. Our image of ourselves physically

We are motivated to make purchases, save, go in debt, based on these self-images. We can be motivated by either the prospect of gain or fear of loss in each of the above areas. Fear of loss is always a stronger motivator.

Let's imagine that I wanted to motivate you to buy life insurance. You are in a comfortable place right now — no health problems, no particular worries. You are in the middle at equilibrium.

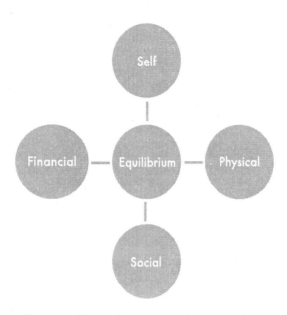

What if I started by asking you a few questions:
If something were to happen to your spouse today and
you had no life insurance — what would be the consequence?
"Gee," you think. "I would need to raise the children on my
own. I don't know how I would cope with taking care of the
baby and working, let alone pay for a funeral. How would my
image of myself change? How would I cope socially? What
effect would the stress have on my health? How would I pay
for child care? So many things would change!"
"Now what about you?" I (your financial planner) continues. "If you didn't have insurance, what would become
of your family? Where would they live? Would they have
enough money to put food on the table and pay the bills? If
not, how does this make you feel?"
"Frankly," you think, "it scares the you know what out of
me." Not feeling so good any more, are you?

Notice that the planner evoked reactions from each of the four motivators. Not knowing exactly which button would set you off, he pushed all of them. As he asks more questions and you provide more answers, he will isolate the factors that will make you most likely to buy.

Some people purchase cheap shoes because it makes them feel thrifty; this is an attribute their parents instilled in them, and their ability to be content with cheap shoes gives them a very positive image of themselves. Others purchase $700 pens and expensive ties because they feel it gives them an edge socially, or perhaps for other reasons related to the four motivators.

I don't think it matters what you buy, but it does matter why you buy. What does that good or service do for you? Are you getting satisfaction from that purchase? Maybe the small stuff does absolutely nothing and adds little value (utils are low); perhaps the small stuff brings significant value (high utils). Most often the things we deem to be of the most worth rarely are the most expensive. Unfortunately many of us dedicate a tremendous amount of time, money and energy chasing after something that disappoints us once we possess it. It's just not all it was cracked up to be.

I was given a quote by a good friend of mine, Mark Bishop, when I was sixteen and have carried it around with me to this day. "You can never get enough of what you don't need, because what you don't need will never satisfy you."

The util meter or satisfaction level we receive from choosing one thing over another comes from the value we attach to it. No one can or should tell you what should be of value to you. But the purchases you make should be consistent with your own values. Sometimes in the short term we make a purchase we think will give us very high utils. As we take some time to think about our recent buy, logic will tell us either we made a choice which was good and consistent with what we value or we will feel that pit in our stomach reminding us that the decision we made was inconsistent with the direction we really wish to go. My worst purchases are those that I don't think about, make on an impulse, and later regret because I didn't take the time to shop, cool off and think through my decision. When we take adequate time to think through our decisions, we will be much more able to satisfy ourselves and our loved ones, because we are choosing to make purchases which are consistent with our values. Therefore we maximize our satisfaction—a dang good thing!

Next time you go shopping, check your "utility meter." If you are not getting value, don't buy it. Maximize your value by choosing items that provide value for today and tomorrow. And remember there are times when you don't need to buy anything; there is a great deal of value and satisfaction to being a saver also. Saving money brings a sense of security, confidence, and hope in the future; this is worth paying for. If you're not sold yet, consider the real life consequences of not saving. Picture your future at age 75. The satisfaction we receive from our money not only brings pleasure, but helps us avoid pain—now and in the future. We must maximize satisfaction with every dollar we bring into the house.

CHAPTER EIGHT

INCREASING PAYMENT FREQUENCY

MOST PEOPLE WHO ARE IN DEBT stay there and rarely move forward, for one simple reason: they pay the minimum amount required by their lender. Credit cards and revolving lines of credit are <u>designed</u> to keep you in debt so the lender can maximize his profit from you — their newest and beloved profit center. Typically a credit card or revolving line of credit requires a monthly installment of 3% of the balance. If we do the math, by paying the minimum 3% on a credit card, the loan would be paid off in 21 years!

Most loans allow us to determine the amount we pay over the minimum required amount and also allow us to increase our payment frequency. On some larger loans we can make payments annually, quarterly, monthly, bi-monthly, bi-weekly, or weekly. Some will allow us to log on and pay as often as daily. Typically the payment frequency on the average loan is preset at monthly, bi-monthly, or bi weekly. What is the difference? Does it really matter? Should you care?

Let's assume you have a loan on which you are making

payments monthly. You would get 12 payments in every year. What if you paid bi-weekly? There are 52 weeks on every year, so you would make 26 half payments. Or 13 full payments. In short, if we make bi-weekly payments we save in 2 areas:

1. The first is that we save time. By making 26 half payments or 13 full payments per year we apply a full extra payment toward the principal. We will save roughly 8 years of payments on a 30 year mortgage.
2. By increasing the frequency, we also decrease the average balance on the loan. By decreasing the average balance, we decrease the interest or carrying charges on the loan and chop it down faster because we are paying less interest.

When I did debt management we used the following analogy. Suppose you were making a monthly furniture payment of $60 per month. Logically, it would not seem to make much difference whether you paid $60 once a month or $2 per day. But it does! If you set it up electronically to pay the lender 30 daily payments of $2, each day you would be reducing the average balance, thus accumulating less interest. In today's computer age, this strategy works wonders. If you simply set up your computer to send $2 per day, every day, you would get very long statements at the end of the month (which would come over the computer anyway) — but your interest costs would be reduced, and you would still paying out about the same amount every month

Can you imagine trying to implement this strategy of increasing payment frequency twenty years ago? Each day we would have to manually write a check for $2, place that check in an envelope, stamp it and mail it off. The costs would kill us and this strategy would be all but impossible.

In today's world we have a significant advantage in that we set it up on our computer once and let it ride. Your monthly printed statement will be longer, but you'll pay off the debt much faster as a greater portion of your payment pays principal because the average daily balance is lower.

Now I have seen some lenders take issue with this strategy. They may tell you that there is far more work in managing your account and they are not "set up to accommodate" this strategy; however, in a computerized world I don't believe this is the case. Really, they don't like the strategy for one reason: it reduces the interest, or revenue generated from you.

Some lenders, in an effort to kibosh this strategy, have taken the position that if you make several smaller payments they will count them as incomplete or partial payments and mark down and report to the credit bureaus that the payment is incomplete even if the total payments are far more than the required minimum.

The bottom line is that it works. Do yourself a favor. Call each of your lenders and ask them how often you can make a payment and set up the payments to come as frequently as possible. Try to move from monthly to biweekly on all payments and watch the balances erode.

Take action today!!!

CHAPTER NINE

SECURED VS. UNSECURED

WHEN A LENDER IS CONSIDERING whether or not to do business with you, one of the main factors other than credit is the collateral you're bringing to the table. In other words, what can the lender take if you don't pay? The best collateral is something they can turn into cash fast. They want security. They want to know that if you don't pay the loan that somehow they can get their money back. If you think about it, it's really quite fair. If I were lending money, I would want to make sure that I would have a good chance of getting my money back.

In very simple terms, the bank can put that money into something very safe like Treasury Bills and they can get a very small return risk free. Everything beyond Treasury Bills has a risk associated to it. If you had $10,000, who would you rather lend the money to — the guy down the street with a steady job, his house paid off, and a good credit rating, or the burned-out bum down the block, with every credit card maxed, who's been out of work for 6 years? While you may like them both equally, you'd have to agree it would make more sense to lend the money to the first guy for 6% and to the second guy for 18%. The higher interest rate is to compensate you for the higher risk you are about to take. In other words there is a much better chance you'll get your money back from the first guy —because he has stuff. If the second guy doesn't pay, what are you going to do? Even if you take him to court, he's got nothing. You can't squeeze blood from a stone; your hard-earned $10,000 is gone and you're out of luck.

Let's talk about two types of loans: secured and unsecured.

Unsecured loans are guaranteed by the general credit of the person borrowing the money — in other word there is no security pledged. When companies borrow money without pledging assets, the loan is called a debenture. If all other factors are equal, interest rates on unsecured loans are always higher because there is a higher risk attached. If the borrower defaults, the lender cannot come after specific assets — they have a far lengthier and much more difficult process to get their money back. The only leverage they have is that they will report the default to your credit agency. Because of this additional risk, the lender will charge a "risk premium" and the rate will be higher.

Secured loans, on the other hand, have a specific asset pledged. For example a mortgage loan is secured by the home; a car loan by the car. If you don't pay the loan they get the property back by selling the home or car. Any equity accumulated along the way is kept by the lender, and this is another way they are compensated for the extra effort and expense required to foreclose the loan. Because collateral is pledged, and they know that no matter what they will get their money back, the risk on this loan is low and consequently the interest rate is much lower.

Not all collateral is treated equally. A small business, for example, may try to offer inventory as collateral. Lenders generally hate inventory. Number one, it's always moving in and out, which makes it difficult for the lender to know how well their loan is secured at any given time. Also, if you don't pay the loan, how are they supposed to sell the inventory? Banks don't want to have to get into the business of trying to sell things they know nothing about. Lenders end up almost giving the inventory away because they don't want to take the time to find out what it is, where to sell it, or who to sell it to. Lenders want something that is easy to turn to cash if the loan goes in the toilet.

J. Paul Getty once said, "If you owe the bank $100, that's your problem. If you owe the bank $100 million, that's the bank's problem." I unfortunately haven't managed to find a banker who's that dumb. I think we'd be hard pressed to have any lender lend $100 million without some type of collateral.

When I take a look at the interest rates of most families, I often find that there are unsecured loans that could be secured. One of the best ways to bring down the interest rate is to secure the loan against collateral. The collateral may be a home, a car or any number of fixed assets. Remember a secured loan has something that is tangible, easy to sell, and has a fairly secure market value.

Here's a story that will give you a chuckle:

Joey, one of my clients' sons, wanted to finance a $7000 stereo through his paper route money. He was short of collateral and wanted to try to get the same rate through the bank as though the loan was secured. In an effort to get a secured loan, he approached the loan officer with a series of hand written IOUs from other friends who incidentally also had no credit. The IOUs indicated a few things:

1. Joey was perceived by his friends to be honest and trustworthy.
2. Joey's friends indicated that if Joey defaulted on the loan, they would take over the payments (and the stereo), and
3. Joey's friends also intended to enjoy the stereo and would pay Joey if he would let them listen.

Joey had it all figured out. He'd hoped he could use these notes as collateral for a better interest rate from the banker. Unfortunately when the bank reviewed the collateral, they couldn't do much with it and had to deny the loan. Joey was out of luck. His dad, however, was thrilled!

I admire what he was trying to accomplish. At his young age he went in with everything he had to negotiate the best possible term for the loan.

Using quality collateral is the key to getting much better rates and terms on loans. Many people who actually have collateral leave personal lines of credit or other bank debt unsecured, incurring a much higher interest rate as a result. When it comes to collateral, first go with the big things — equity in a home, stock certificates, or a car. Next get creative; antiques, paintings, stamp, or coin collections — anything that would be of value to a bank.

Don't tell yourself it's not worth it, because all these little things do add up. Shaving just 1% off the interest rate on a $100,000 mortgage will save $24,755 over the course of a 30 year loan. That's a big deal! And you <u>will</u> save at least 1% with good collateral. Take a look at what loans are currently outstanding and see what equity you could pledge. It may be possible to drop the rate a couple of percentage points and put money in your pocket!

CHAPTER TEN

PLANNING YOUR PURCHASES

YESTERDAY I MET WITH A YOUNG COUPLE name Shannon and Dave. They were recent college graduates in the second year of their careers, and just had their first child. As I went through their financial information, a cold deep pit sank into my stomach. When they first graduated and began to work full time, they felt liberated that they were finally no longer living off student loans; they thought they were finally in the position to pay their own bills and make some financial headway. With their new sense of freedom came new purchases: a home, new furnishings, a celebration vacation, a new computer, a new video camera, and unfortunately car repairs. Because they were not used to paying taxes, they neglected funds for tax savings and had unpaid taxes overdue. They both sat in front of me in a stupor. "How could it be that we are as tight financially as we were as students when we are making money now? When will we be rid of this constant financial pressure? Have we come so far down that we can never get back on top? Please help!" As you can tell a great deal of emotion and little thought went into the new purchases and now they had to dig their way out of this hole.

In contrast, two of my best clients, John and Vickie earn a decent living — $55K a year each. They are one of the few couples out there with a 20 year game plan. This game plan is built much the way a general contractor builds a building.

Building plans include a timetable detailing where material is purchased, when it's delivered, which contractors are hired and at what cost. Sequencing is crucial to the success of the operation. Having the drywallers come in before the framers would create frustrated drywallers and a goofy looking building. The framers, plumbers, painters, carpenters, and electricians must all work in sequence.

The delivery of materials must also coincide with the trade doing the work. If these items are not coordinated, building costs would skyrocket; disorganization and frustration would ensue. In short, you'd get a shoddy building at three times the price that wouldn't hold up through a windstorm.

John and Vickie have a timetable for every major purchase they plan to make over the next 20 years. In their plan they have outlined when they plan to upgrade their home, do major renovations, pay for children's education, purchase vehicles, and take vacations.

They also do their homework to try and get a rough idea for what they plan to spend in each area. For example, the couple determined that they needed two vehicles, and they felt that they would be able to drive each vehicle for eight years. Every four years they planned to replace one vehicle. They would always have a relatively new vehicle to take on road trips and one that was ready to retire.

They outlined where they wanted to go on vacations and

GET YOURSELF OUT OF DEBT NOW!

which areas of the world they wanted to see. They anticipated which home expenses to expect, and where and how they would renovate their home to meet their needs over the years. Then they did something amazing. They set up five different accounts and named them. One account was called the new vehicle fund, another the vacation fund. They decided to save in advance for every major purchase and set up monthly contributions to each account. When the purchases were made, they were treated like a reward for their patience and efforts in savings. They made a decision that they were going to do their very best to have interest work for them instead of always against them. Their goal was to either pay for each expenditure in cash or put as much as they could down to lower their monthly payment and free up cash flow. Even though they may not have always been able to fund the entire amount up front, they were able to come pretty close.

As the time nears for John and Vickie to make a major purchase, they begin to fill in more details in their plan. About three months before buying a car, for example, they shop the market to get a clear view on what would best serve their family. Then they further narrow their choices by comparison shopping for features and benefits, and finally shopping for price.

What I like most about their plan and their personalities is that they are not impulse buyers. They have a conscious strategy for determining how to make the best use of their resources and they do not make their decisions based on emotion or fad chasing.

When I looked at John and Vickie's debt obligations on a monthly basis, the numbers were very low. This in turn gave them a lower debt servicing ratio, and more favorable terms if they ever need to finance. The analogy I like to use is taking a canoe down the river. When the boat is light it moves easily and getting to the destination requires minimal effort. When the boat is weighed down by debt, reaching the destination is much more difficult and requires far more effort. John and Vickie are riding with a light boat. The young couple, on the other hand, is so weighed down with debt they are paddling hard just to stay afloat; making financial headway under those circumstances is very hard.

Now I know what you are thinking. "Wow, that seems like a lot of work!" Or "I don't like being that disciplined," or worse yet, "I'd rather just shoot from the hip." My argument would be: try to construct a building with that attitude and I'd get a kick out of seeing what it looks like.

Certainly not all the uncertainties of life can be mapped out in this way. Unemployment, disability, illness, inheritance, significant pay raises, and other misfortunes and windfalls happen to us all. It would not be possible for most of us to have every item orchestrated. But it is possible, and desirable, to establish a rough idea of where you're trying to go with your life, and set goals and deadlines to get what you want by having interest work on your side instead of against you.

The planning is simple. First we need to determine what we want, then build a plan to get it through saving a little every month. We have anything we want if we work towards it. In the words of Larry Winget, "What I think about, talk about, and do something about, comes about." Start working on your plan today!

CHAPTER ELEVEN

APPRECIATING VS. DEPRECIATING ASSETS

I'VE HAD CLIENTS ASK, "Are there any circumstances under which incurring debt is okay?" Definitely, the best example would be education. Education does a tremendous amount to increase the amount of future earnings potential. There are, however, many ways to get and enhance an education. Some choose years of formal education through university, college, or trade or technical schools. Without question formal education opens doors and is a wonderful tool to help you navigate through life. Those with an education, on average, earn far more throughout their life than with someone without it.

There is also informal education — learning through experience. Trial and error and the school of hard knocks can teach practical lessons often not gained through class room theory. If this is your game plan, success will require far more effort and a bit more luck.

The cost of education, therefore, should be viewed as an investment in yourself.

In other words, you're most valuable asset is your capacity to earn income. Investing and reinvesting in yourself is vital! And frankly I'm astonished at how much we invest in other things and how little we spend on personal development. Education should never end. Throughout our working lives, we should be attending courses so we can bring more to the table for our business, customers or employer. We've all seen those who have stopped developing; it's only a matter of time before current skill sets are obsolete and you're getting replaced by younger and less experienced people who have been trained on the latest software, methods or approaches. No one can afford to stop investing in themselves, whether formally or informally. Education pays huge dividends and appreciates your value and your ability earn a living for yourself.

The second item for which most people take a loan is a home. Real estate generally appreciates; which means if you buy a home for $100K when the value goes up — and generally always does-- you are the beneficiary building equity and net worth. I love appreciating assets!

I really don't have a problem with taking a loan to buy a home as long as the payment is within your means. And I mean well within your means. I have to laugh seeing these young couples who are still hanging bedsheets in their front windows because they cannot afford blinds. They've put the minimum down to get into the house, gotten the shortest term variable rate, falsified and inflated their income to buy what is really outside of their price range and are praying that the interest rates don't move so it doesn't come crumbling down.

The liabilities that scare me are the depreciating ones — assets that become less valuable the longer they are held.

Some good examples of depreciating assets are cars, furniture, or consumer debt. When you take a loan on a new car and drive it off of the lot, immediately 30% of the value of the car is gone. Yet you still owe the full value of the loan. Over a period of time the car depreciates rapidly until it's worthless. A new car usually takes about 7-10 years before its worth almost nothing. I find it interesting that there are many who are very comfortable taking a loan knowing that the moment they drive they car from the lot they will owe 30% more than what the vehicle is worth.

What's worse is consumer debt! Suppose I didn't have money to pay for dinner so I charged it on my credit card, knowing I would not have the immediate funds to pay it off. What I am doing is taking a loan and once the meal is finished the value of that meal is gone — it's worthless. So I am carrying a debt with no assets to compliment the loan on my balance sheet. Taking out a loan on a car was bad enough, because I immediately lost 30%; however, the meal was worthless as soon as I swallowed the last bite.

The rate at which an asset depreciates is important. What is more important is whether we can get the asset to appreciate or grow in value. These types of loans are much easier to justify. This is why I am baffled by the attitude of people who assert they would never take a loan for the purpose of investing — too aggressive, they say. However, a balanced pool of investments always goes up — at least this is what history tells us. Investments appreciate in value if the investments are held for long term. Yet these same people blithely take out a loan for a car, which is bound to depreciate! I don't get it.

Whenever we take on a debt, or any obligation to pay in the future, we should have an asset of equivalent value. We should also have an expectation that the asset purchased will rise in value. Why would we sacrifice our future for something that is going to be worth less?

I firmly believe God wants us to have all of the wonderful things of this world. We demonstrate our reliability with the stewardships we have been granted. Stewardship or the demonstration of responsibility is a very interesting thing. If we manage small amounts properly, we demonstrate our trustworthiness and will be given larger amounts. This is exactly why most lottery winners are in worse shape seven years after winning their lotto than they would have been had they never won. In almost all cases these lotto winners have not developed the skills to manage, and hence, keep their money.

I recently heard a story of a lottery winner in Halifax, Nova Scotia who won $10 million dollars. After seven years of wine, women, and song he was completely broke. For the first time in seven years he had to go looking for work. His friend found him a job in the heavy equipment business. He was so disgusted with himself he committed suicide.

Throw the thoughts aside of winning big, MLM payoffs, or the latest Internet scam. There is no shortcut to success. The road to success is paved with blood, sweat, tears, and long hours. The faint of heart need not apply.

So remember: when you think about borrowing money, consider whether your asset will appreciate or depreciate. Remember, this is over the long term. If we were to appraise the value of any home, we would expect its market value to fluctuate significantly from quarter to quarter. Over the long term, however — ten or twenty years — the chances of real estate going up are very, very, good. In this case I'm not worried about carrying a loan on the property because history shows us that a home will almost always appreciate in value.

There's one more thing to consider: how liquid your asset is. In other words, if you get into trouble, how quickly can you sell the asset without losing your shirt? If the asset is hard to sell, you may be stuck with it for months and forced to make payments, pay taxes, and advertising expenses until you can get rid if it. This is why staying on the conservative side of the line always pays; it protects your cash flow. By protecting cash flow we are able to save more, as opposed to having to rely on credit to carry us through the thin periods.

Donald Trump provides an interesting example of using appreciating assets to his advantage. At any given moment, he is billions of dollars in debt. However, on the balance sheet he has corresponding appreciating assets as collateral. What Trump does is use someone else's money, and gets others to service his debt through rents or other income he receives. This way he can be the beneficiary of market appreciation. This strategy carries a tremendous amount of risk with a corresponding incredible reward. Getting into debt is not magic; any idiot can do that. The magic is using debt as a tool to leverage appreciating assets effectively while appropriately managing cash flow. If you can master this, you've got the world by the tail.

But always be sure to protect your cash flow! If cash flow is chewed up by servicing depreciating or depreciated debt, you can get into big trouble fast. We first must pay depreciating debt off as quickly as possible.

So before you decide to take out a loan, consider a couple of things:

1. Is cash flow stable and sufficient to handle the repayment schedule?
2. Will the asset appreciate or depreciate in value?
3. How liquid is the asset — how hard will it be to sell if necessary?

We all need to buy things which depreciate — we all buy food, gas, furniture, cars, etc. Just don't take out a loan to pay for them! If the asset will appreciate in value, feel free to take out a loan to pay for it as long as it fits into cash flow, both immediately and in the future.

CHAPTER TWELVE

THE ENTREPRENEURIAL SPIRIT

IT IS A SAD FACT that over half of the families coming to the table with bankruptcy or debt management issues are entrepreneurs. Small business owners and struggling farmers often have every dime invested and reinvested back into their business. They are sometimes referred to as asset rich, cash flow poor. Fledgling entrepreneurs put every penny back in the business to help the venture get on its feet. This always seems to take twice the money, twice the time and yield half the payout the entrepreneur expects. Yet unless mommy and daddy are loaded and our entrepreneur has a free ride to the top, this evolution of the business is vital. It teaches you to build a business and sustain it. The personal refining that takes place during the evolution of a business builds great business people.

Entrepreneurs building a business sacrifice a great deal. They risk the initial and ongoing investments into the business, and risk continues to be ever-present. Five out of seven businesses bite the dust in the first year, yet the freedom, profit, and sense of personal pride make starting a business very worthwhile for those that make it.

Before I go further, I think it important to recognize what risk is. Taking a risk is not the same as being a gambler. Gamblers are stupid people — the odds are stacked against them. Gamblers are those that roll the dice and let fate define their futures. Unfortunately, many people enter a business this way. They arrive with no skills, no plan, no cash, and little concept of what is takes to make this type of business a success. This is not risk taking — this is gambling.

Wise philosophers tell us to "know thyself." All growth begins with a rigorous self-examination. Before you start a business, you must be honest with yourself and objectively look at your skills and strengths.

What skills do you bring to the table? Are you a good marketer, money manager, sales closer, or technician? Do you like to be out in front or behind the scenes? A business needs all these qualities. If you're running a business on your own, then you have to fill all those hats whether you like it or not. At my office we say if you don't have an assistant, you are one.

By honestly determining what you bring to the table, you can hire staff to round out the skill sets where you fall short. This is difficult for many entrepreneurs, who try to micromanage every detail of their business. These control freaks just can't let other people assume responsibilities for the details and spend obscene hours trying to do it all, because they think that no one can do it better than they can. They're wrong — and they will stay broke until they can delegate the "stuff" and focus on the income-generating activities. As your business grows, you reach a point where you must hire others to perform all the tasks you don't do well, and then you can focus on the activities that bring in the coin.

For example, when the band The Rolling Stones started they did everything: booking, advertising, contract negotiation, equipment set up, lights, and wardrobe — as well as writing and performing their music. They recognized, however, that their unique ability was musical. This is what the people came to see. Even though they may have enjoyed the setup or advertising, this is not where the money was, and they were exhausting themselves by trying to do it all. As their business evolved they delegated everything else but their unique ability. All they do now is show up and play. Every great business must go through this evolution — even The Rolling Stones.

Some entrepreneurs' problem is even more basic; they sincerely don't seem to know what business they are in. In Canada we have an airline called Air Canada, perhaps the worst-run business I have ever seen. They simply don't know who they are. Every time a new competitor emerges, they reinvent themselves. They have had new offshoots, called Tango, Jazz, Jetz, etc. If any other airline comes out with a new idea or program, they are on the bandwagon again.

Mercedes does not have an emergency board meeting whenever Yugo announces they are coming to market with a new car. They recognize where they compete — the luxury car market. Who cares what Yugo does? From Mercedes' perspective, Yugo is not their competition. Air Canada tries to fight battles they shouldn't be in the first place. The company has always marketed itself as the premium airline — the best of the best. If that's true, they don't need to compete with discounts. You can't be all things to everyone. Know who you are, know who your competition is, and then you can compete and win. You can't fight on all fronts and be successful.

Also, beware of billing yourself as the low cost provider, because this only allows you one feature to compete on, and you're going head to head with others who have deeper pockets. I love being a premium provider. You can compete on service, quality, store cleanliness, etc.

While I was in Safeway last week, I overheard the deli clerk complaining to her associate that their groceries are more expensive than the discount place down the street. I thought to myself, "Of course the discount store is cheaper, you dummy! That's what a discount store is!" But over there you can't find a thing, you have to bag your own groceries, no one helps you to the car, their deli, meat department and bakery have no service—of course they are cheaper. They should be cheaper! But I shop here because of the extra amenities, and if the cost is higher so what? Nothing good is cheap and nothing cheap is good!!! Quality is worth paying for! If all we wanted were the cheapest options, we would live in cardboard boxes and eat tree bark! People should and will pay for service, quality and value, and Safeway knows this.

As a new entrepreneur, you need some reasonable expectations for your business. Where will clients come from? How much can you earn per client? How many clients do you need to earn a living? What are our margins? What are our costs, both fixed and variable? Who do we know that's already doing this, and what pitfalls could they help us avoid? What could they teach us? What will our startup costs likely be? Where can we get the money? What is our budget? How will we handle marketing? What centers of influence could help us get this business off the ground? You'll never get all the answers you need, but the goal is to get as many answers as you can; these questions paint a picture and help us get a clearer understanding of what this business will look like. This exercise is very valuable! Why do you want to be an entrepreneur? My friend Brian Mennis says, "People are always running to something or away from it." There are all kinds of bad reasons for starting a business: an inability to get along with anyone, an overwhelming desire to be in control, a lack of skills, a lack of work ethic. People who fit those descriptions have no hope of ever running a profitable business.

There are also many incredible people who would be great entrepreneurs! The formula to success is simple and difficult — the right idea, the willingness and ability to build a plan, then the effort to work the right idea into a successful profitable business. With those attributes, you could make millions!

We must start with a very clear picture of what we want, determine what effort is required to get it, and then resolve to pay the price to get it. This commitment you make to yourself is non-negotiable.

How do you manage a new business' cash flow? Starting a new business is like working on commission. The first couple of months the income is nothing, then $8,000, then $2,000, then $10,000, then zero and constantly up and down. Later the ups and downs get higher and higher until managing the business gets easier and easier.

When managing cash flow that is to be used for personal use, this can be very difficult. If you let your fluctuating income determine your lifestyle, one month you'll be buying pricey toys, spending thousands of dollars, and living high off of the hog — next month you're living on cat food and hoping the mortgage check doesn't bounce.

The key is to put all of the money into a personal savings or money market account. Then at the beginning of every month, write yourself a check as though you were on salary. This evens out the windfalls and deserts and keeps the ulcers and the grey hair away. When you find that you're building up a significant amount, you now know it's time to give yourself a bonus, increase your salary, or dump a lump sum into more long term investments. Whatever option you choose, keeping a 3-6 month cushion is essential and keeps the dogs from the door.

CHAPTER THIRTEEN

MAKE IT LAST, WEAR IT OUT, MAKE IT DO, OR DO WITHOUT

WHEN I WAS ABOUT 10, I loved to visit my great-grandparents at the lake. Grandpa Louis always had some kind of job he'd been saving for our arrival. On one such occasion, as I was pounding a nail into a piece of wood, the nail bent. Assuming it was ruined I yanked it out and reached over to grab another. To my surprise my great-grandfather picked up the nail and taught me how to straighten and reuse it. To this day I straighten bent nails as a personal reminder of how carefully and thoughtfully he used his resources.

I was born in 1973 and have three brothers. As I child I can distinctly remember the iron-on knee patches my mom would put on our pants as my brothers and I would tear through another pair. My mom made a point of helping us wear out our clothes in an effort to maximize their use and value to the family.

As I look at the past year and a half, it's amazing to see

the technology I've gone through. My cell phone provider phoned me to offer me a new phone at no cost as they were upgrading their system; there was nothing wrong with my old phone, but I took him up on his offer. Six months later I upgraded to a Treo phone with a Palm Pilot. Three months later my son threw the phone on the ground and cracked the screen; I've upgraded several times since then and now onto my third Blackberry. A new model has just come out with some useful features and already I'm considering upgrading.

One of the keys to wealth is to "make it last, wear it out, make it do or do without," and that is a hard thing to do. As we've become more prosperous as a society, more of what we own becomes disposable. When I was a child, the norm was to drive the same vehicle for at least eight years; now we lease them. We want a new vehicle in the driveway every three or four years.

Are we trying to impress the neighbors, keep up with the latest style or technology advance, or do we just like new stuff? I don't know what the answer is, but I know I'm guilty of it. Incidentally, a recent study showed that people who drive their cars for eight years retire an average of six years earlier than the norm. Frugality pays in unexpected ways.

The moral is to make certain we exhaust the use and value before we trash it. One of the keys to financial prosperity is to use resources effectively and to make the most of the resource we have. We must get away from the disposable nature of our resources and find ways to consume less by using and reusing what we already have.

So much of this hits home as common sense; the goal is to make it common practice. Principles of financial management in and of themselves mean nothing unless they are applied to our daily lives. I challenge you to revisit the use of resources in your household; I'm going to try to do the same in mine.

CHAPTER FOURTEEN

WORK WITH A CERTIFIED FINANCIAL PLANNER

IN MY CURRENT ROLE, I direct a team of financial planners. In a meeting I was conducting the rhetorical question was asked, "Why use a financial planner?" My first thought was, "Why don't we build our own cars, why don't we do our own dentistry, why don't we make our own clothes, why don't we install our own carpet?"

The answer to me is a simple one: we could! If we really wanted to, we could. I could install the carpet in my home and I can see the look on my wife's face when I show her the results. The look on her face would say loud and clear, "I don't want to hurt your feelings, honey, but that really looks like crap!" We don't make our own cars or do our own dentistry for the same reason.

Hopefully we realize that not every person can be an expert at everything. Despite knowing this, many still try to be their own financial advisor. No training, no understanding of how investments work, no comprehension of how betas and correlation patterns fit (or what they are), no insight into taxation or estate planning, no clue where their retirement income will come from. I imagine your financial plan looks like my carpet. One hell of a mess!

How, then, can we be surprised that only 4% or Americans or Canadians are retiring wealthy? Did you know that only 17% of senior citizens can meet their obligations and the rest are financially dependent on others? In the wealthiest countries in the world that is ridiculous. If you think you are saving money by not working with a planner, you're kidding yourself. You may be looking at spending your golden years at the Golden Arches.

Choosing a planner is not easy and finding a good one that is trustworthy and competent may be hard. Start with the CFP designation. This Certified Financial Planner designation says that they have proven competence through courses taken and passed, they have agreed to abide by a code of ethics, and they are required to upgrade skills regularly through continuing education credits.

Next is personality. Find a planner that speaks to you in a language you can understand. Like any profession, some planners like to confuse others by throwing out industry terminology only a few understand in an effort to make themselves sound more sophisticated than they are.

A milk stool requires three legs to stand; if any leg is missing, the stool will tip over. Do the milk stool test on your potential financial planner. Here are the three legs or questions you should ask: Do you trust this person? Do you like this person? If you were having the President of your company over for dinner, would this be the type of person you would feel comfortable having there? A yes to all three questions indicates someone you can work with.

When the planner you choose does a good job for you, refer them to everyone you know. Your friends and family should be entitled to benefit as you have. Being retired and golfing alone is not nearly as fun as having your family and friends there with you. And don't you want your friends to realize the thousands of dollars in interest saved and investments built by avoiding the pitfalls of poor financial planning?

I've heard it said that nothing matters until it really matters, and then nothing else matters. A financial plan is certainly a great example of this adage. You need a reliable financial planner to help you design a plan that makes sense for you and your family.

What should a financial plan include? A Will, to begin with. Wills can get very complex or can stay very simple. At the very least they should have an executor, or executrix and a guardian for your children. An executor files your last tax return, pays off debts, settles debts owed to you and the list continues depending upon where you live. This person must be someone you trust.

The consequences are clear when it comes to not having a guardian appointed for your children. The child will be awarded to the province or state; it then becomes the responsibility of family and friends to step up and apply for guardianship. If this is scaring you, it should; it scares me, as I believe it is the responsibility of parents to protect their children. If you don't have a will, get one made now.

Nothing matters until it really matters, and then that's all that matters.

Next is disability insurance. In many respects, this is more important than life insurance. One out of every three people is on disability at some point in their life. The disability averages 2.9 years. If you or I became disabled today, would we get paid, how much would we be paid, and under what conditions would we be paid? Nothing matters, until it really matters, and then that's all that matters.

You should have life insurance. Your life insurance plan should include two things: cash and income replacement. In my family for example, I am the main breadwinner and my wife is home with our children. If something were to happen to me today, she would need cash to pay for a funeral, pay off debts, tuck money away for the kids' educations, and donate to charity. The second thing she needs is an ongoing income. We add up all of the cash needs, add up all of the income replacement needs, and come up with a number. This is called an insurance needs analysis and should be completed with a CFP and licensed insurance agent. As far as I'm concerned parents who have young children and refuse to get life insurance are irresponsible parents. Nothing matters, until it really matters, and then that's all that matters.

Next is debt management, and what can I say about this — you've just read a whole book about it. Nothing matters, until it really matters, and then that's all that matters.

You'll need to think about retirement planning and investment management. Whether it is the kids' education, buying the next vehicle or developing a retirement plan, you must think about your future. How will these future things be financed? The closer the event, the clearer your need becomes. Retirement planning for most families will require a lifetime of savings and your financial planner should be able to give you an indication of how much you will need and where your income will come from when the date arrives. We all know families who didn't plan properly, don't we? With the use of the expertise of a financial planner, you can avoid the pitfalls that come to those who didn't take action. Nothing matters until it really matters, and then that's all that matters.

Life is about balance — enjoying today and tomorrow. Making decisions based on true principles will lead you to every success faster and with greater ease. I wish you the very best as you understand where you are and where you want to be, set your goals, and build and execute your plan for a brighter today and tomorrow.

Warmest regards,

Jamie Vermeeren

ISBN 142518622-X